Family Night Lessons to Prepare Your Child for Baptism

Alison Palmer

CURRAWONG PRESS

Currawong Press books are available through
Deseret Book Distributors
57 W. South Temple
Salt Lake City, Utah 84101

ISBN: 978-1-59992-910-1

Contents

Introduction

Preparing for baptism is an exciting time in a child's life. It also offers a wonderful opportunity for the family to review the basic doctrines of the Church, the elements of their own testimonies, and the covenants they made at baptism.

This family home evening manual is designed to help families draw closer to each other and to the Lord as they support a child in preparing for baptism. You may also want to use these lessons to help new investigators or converts understand the gospel, or any other time you need a quick and fun way to spend time with your family.

To help make these lessons as stress-free as possible, there is a minimum amount of preparation, and most of the supplies are items you will already have in your home. Use the *Gospel Art Book* (available at store.lds.org) for the suggested illustrations, and look to the additional resources for fun stories, games, coloring pages, puzzles, and videos to enhance your time together.

Enjoy your family, and enjoy the blessings of the gospel!

Our Loving Heavenly Father

Scripture

Psalm 82:6

Song

"My Heavenly Father Loves Me," *Children's Songbook*, 228

Preparation

Gather a pencil and a sheet of paper for each member of the family. You will also need a favorite picture of Jesus Christ (see *Gospel Art Book* for ideas).

Lesson

Discuss the ways earthly parents can show and express love for their children. How does this compare to the ways Heavenly Father shows us love?

Pass out the sheets of paper and ask each family member to draw a picture of himself or herself. When everyone is finished, spend a few minutes talking about the characteristics shared by members of the family, such as brown hair, green eyes, or freckles.

Next, have the family turn their papers over and write or draw a few things about themselves that aren't as visible from the outside, such as "likes animals," "happy," or "patient." Talk about the many types of things family members can have in common. These things help them understand and love each other more.

Ask the family for their impressions of the phrase "I am a child of God." What thoughts come to mind? How does the knowledge that we are children of Heavenly Father make your family members feel about themselves? Remind them that when we left Heavenly

Father to come to earth, each of us was given a physical body and placed in a family where we could learn and grow to be like Him. In addition to our body, we have a spirit. Heavenly Father has a body and spirit as well. Here on earth, not all of our bodies look the same, and not all of our spirits have the same talents or gifts, but we all possess goodness and blessings given to us by a loving Heavenly Father to help us understand Him, love Him, and learn how to return to Him.

As an example, show the family your picture of the Savior. Ask the family to share some of the things they love best about Him. Point out attributes they mention that have also been listed on their own papers. Discuss how our blessings and the godly attributes we see in ourselves and others can help us understand how much Heavenly Father and the Savior love us. Talk about the ways we can show love, reverence, and respect for Them in return. Discuss proper reverence for the names of Heavenly Father and Jesus Christ.

End by reminding family members that they are children of God, that He loves each of us, and that He has a plan for our happiness that will help us return to Him. When we seek out the best parts of ourselves and our families, we are following that plan and showing how much we love Him as well.

Activity

Invite each family member to use pictures from old magazines to create a collage of their favorite things and their blessings from Heavenly Father.

Treat

Divinity Fudge

3 cups sugar
½ cup corn syrup
⅔ cup water

2 egg whites

¼ teaspoon vanilla

1 cup chopped pecans

1. Combine sugar, syrup, and water in a microwavable container. Heat the mixture in the microwave on high for 12 to 18 minutes, until a droplet of the mixture spins a thin thread when dropped into water.
2. While the sugar is cooking, whip the eggs whites and salt until stiff peaks form.
3. Continue whipping the egg whites while gradually adding the hot sugar mixture. The combined ingredients will thicken further.
4. Add the vanilla and nuts. Drop by the spoonful onto parchment paper and let the treats cool completely.

Additional Resources

Boyd K. Packer, "Who Is Heavenly Father?" *Friend*, Feb. 2012. https://www.lds.org/friend/2012/02/who-is-heavenly-father?lang=eng

M. Russell Ballard, "How do I know that Heavenly Father loves Me?" *Friend*, Aug. 2009. https://www.lds.org/friend/2009/08/how-do-i-know-that-heavenly-father-loves-me?lang=eng

"I Am My Heavenly Father's Child," *Liahona*, Feb. 2005. http://www.lds.org/liahona/2005/02/i-am-my-heavenly-fathers-child?lang=eng

"Heavenly Father Loves You," *Friend*, Mar. 2003. http://www.lds.org/friend/2003/03/heavenly-father-loves-you?lang=eng

The Earthly Ministry of Jesus Christ

Scripture

2 Nephi 31:7

Song

"He Sent His Son," *Children's Songbook*, 34

Preparation

Have a *Gospel Art Book* available, as well as a candle for each member of the family, and some matches or a lighter.

Lesson

Darken the room as much as possible, then light a single candle. Talk about all the things the flame can represent—beauty, warmth, light, etc. Ask the family if they think the candle would give enough light to help you walk through the room. Would it be able to guide everyone in the family at the same time? Though the flame from the candle might be bright enough to help one person to find his or her way out of a dark room, it would not provide enough light for more than one person to find the way.

Give each family member his or her own candle. If your children are still small, sit them around a table where the candle can rest in front of them without them holding it. Go around the room and light the other candles. Discuss the difference multiple candles can make to the darkness in a room and for a person's confidence if he or she needed to use that light to find the way.

After the candles have been safely extinguished, lead the family into a discussion of the uses of fire and light in terms of gospel symbolism. Jesus Christ is our light and our lifeline to eternal life. He is the Light of the World. His life on earth showed us how we should live our own lives. We look to Him in order to find our way through our trials and problems.

Jesus Christ has asked us to nurture the flame of our testimonies and to use that light to help others. We cannot depend on another person's light to give us enough direction and strength to make it back to Heavenly Father. We each need to find our own testimony to light our way. When we carry our own light and are surrounded by others who share their light with us, it is easier for us to live the gospel, to withstand our trials, and to make it back to Heavenly Father.

Ask the family to share ideas on how a person might find and light his or her own flame of testimony. How is that flame nurtured?

Hand out sheets of paper so that each family member can draw a picture portraying his or her favorite story about Jesus Christ. Have each person share the picture, tell the story, and explain what makes it his or her favorite.

Discuss why it is so important to learn all we can about the Savior. Look through the *Gospel Art Book* together and point out additional stories and life lessons that can be obtained from them.

Emphasize that since Jesus Christ is the original source of the light we carry or have within us, learning about Him and committing to following His example is the best way to keep our personal testimony lit. The more we learn about Him, the more desire we will have to be like Him, and the brighter our testimony will shine.

Emphasize your desire for each child to find and nurture his or her own testimony of the Savior. Testify of Him and encourage each person to think about Him every day. They can ponder what they love most about Him, just as they did with the pictures they drew.

Activity

Play charades with familiar stories from Christ's life. Divide the family into two teams and take turns silently acting out the chosen story for the other team to guess.

Treat

Loaves and Fishes

4 English muffins
8 slices American cheese
2 cans tuna fish, drained
½ cup mayonnaise
2 tablespoons onion
2 tablespoons pickle relish

1. Split and toast the English muffins.
2. Combine tuna, mayo, onion, and pickle relish in a bowl.
3. Top each muffin half with the tuna salad, then cover the salad with a slice of cheese.
4. Place the open-faced tuna melts onto a baking tray and broil just until the cheese is melted.

Additional Resources

Dieter F. Uchtdorf, "Becoming Like Jesus Christ," *Friend,* Jan. 2009. http://www.lds.org/friend/2009/01/becoming-like-jesus-christ?lang=eng

"He Lives: Testimonies of Jesus Christ," lds.org. http://www.lds.org/pages/he-lives-testimonies?lang=eng

"Jesus Christ Feeds 5,000," *Friend,* Mar. 2013. http://media.ldscdn.org/pdf/magazines/friend-march-2013/2013-03-23-coloring-page-eng.pdf

The Atonement

Scripture

John 3:16

Song

"Help Us, O God, to Understand," *Children's Songbook*, 73

Preparation

Set aside a picture of the Savior (see *Gospel Art Book* for ideas) and a picture of an infant. Find a broken object in your home. This can be as simple as a worn sock or a missing button, or more complicated, like a broken lamp or a bicycle tire that is flat. Make sure you have materials on hand to repair the item.

Lesson

Show the broken object and discuss it with your family. Let them participate in fixing the object. Compare the repaired item to its original state and its broken one. Can you still tell the item was broken? Is the family proud of their solution and their work in repairing the item? What else did they learn from the experience?

Remind the family that we came to earth to grow and be tested. Heavenly Father wants us to learn how to be happy and return to Him. Show the picture of the infant. An infant does not come to earth knowing how to do everything it needs to grow and survive. The baby is given help from those who love him or her. Even so, there will be times when things go wrong. Talk about what happens when the infant learns to walk. It takes time, a number of falls, and sometimes cuts and bruises before the child can stand tall, run, and walk as Heavenly Father intended him or her to. Even then, falls can still happen along the way.

As we learn and grow, we face times when our bodies or our spirits are bruised or broken. Heavenly Father knew these times would come, so He sent His Son to earth to atone for our sins. Jesus Christ wanted to do this because He loves us. Show the picture of the Savior. His suffering in the Garden of Gethsemane, His death on the hill of Calvary, and His Resurrection help us as we learn to obey Heavenly Father. Because Jesus Christ suffered for our sins, He understands how we feel after we break one of His commandments. During the Atonement, He also experienced all of the feelings and problems each of us will have during our mortal life. This allows Him to know exactly how to help us when we are sad or sick or just having a difficult time.

Explain how olives are pressed in order to remove the oil, which is used in many things we eat, and for other purposes. In the scriptures, Christ says that He has trodden the wine-press alone (see Isaiah 63:3). Tell the children that this means that He alone atoned for our sins.

The Savior's Atonement allows us to be resurrected and live forever. He can help us repair our lives and hearts when we make mistakes or do things that are wrong. As we make righteous choices, repent, and do our best to keep the commandents, the Atonement gives us the power and ability to fix our life and spirit—to become better. Review the steps of repentance and how they help in the healing process. You may also want to discuss the emotions and difficulties associated with the process.

Testify of the Atonement and Resurrection of the Savior, and His vital role in making us whole and new again so we can return to Heavenly Father. Jesus Christ loves us more than we can ever imagine. After we have done everything we can to repent of our sins and fix our mistakes, He can make us new again, just as if we had never been broken. Express your gratitude for everything the Savior has done for you and your family.

Activity

If you know someone who restores old furniture or works with antiques, invite that person to share his or her talent with your family. Otherwise, teach your children how to do the laundry, including experimenting with different ways to remove stains from clothing. Hint: as a reward for the children's work, let them use the laundry baskets as sleds on the stairs or snow, or use bed sheets that are drying to build forts.

Treat

Buy or make a veggie pizza with extra olives.

Additional Resources

"The Atonement" *Friend*, Mar. 1995. https://www.lds.org/friend/1995/03/the-atonement?lang=eng

Laurel Rohlfing, "Sharing Time: The Atonement," *Friend*, Mar. 1989. https://www.lds.org/friend/1989/03/sharing-time-the-atonement?lang=eng

Karen Ashton, "Sharing Time: Jesus Christ's Atonement Is the Greatest Gift of Love," *Friend*, Feb. 1996. http://www.lds.org/friend/1996/02/sharing-time-jesus-christs-atonement-is-the-greatest-gift-of-love?lang=eng

"Matt and Mandy: We Will Live Again," *Friend*, Mar. 2009. http://www.lds.org/friend/online-activities/videos/matt-mandy?lang=eng#we-will-live-again

The Holy Ghost

Scripture

John 14:26–27

Song

"The Still Small Voice," *Children's Songbook*, 106

Preparation

Place a copy of John 14:26–27 in an envelope for use during the lesson. You will need pens, tape, five or six sheets of blank paper, and a stack of index cards. Write situations that are pertinent to your family on the sheets of paper. These should include decisions to be made and times when protection or comfort may be needed.

Lesson

Begin by asking the family to try to identify the sound of different instruments in a piece of music. It takes practice to separate one sound from another and to identify each one. We can learn to hear the voice of the Lord—the Holy Ghost—just as we can learn to identify the sounds of different instruments.

Choose two family members to play a game of hot and cold to help you introduce the lesson. Ask one person to leave the room, and have the other hide the prepared scripture envelope. Invite the first person back in and instruct him or her to listen as the other person whispers to help him or her locate the hidden object. The family member who hid the card cannot move from an assigned spot. The other person must listen carefully for the whispers of "warm," "hot," or "cold" as he or she moves around the room looking for the object.

When the envelope has been retrieved, ask the family to share their thoughts on what you will be discussing in family home evening. Have someone read the scripture from the envelope to confirm the subject matter.

Explain that after we are baptized, we are confirmed a member of the Church and receive the gift of the Holy Ghost. This gift is the ability to have the Spirit with us always if we are obedient to Heavenly Father's commandments.

Ask the family to share what they already know about the Holy Ghost and His role in our lives. Explain that the Holy Ghost is the Spirit of God and is often referred to simply as the Spirit. Discuss some of His other titles in the scriptures, such as the Comforter and the Testifier. His promptings are sometimes referred to as the "still small voice." Why is it important to listen to Him? Expand your discussion using information from the entry "Holy Ghost" in the Bible Dictionary.

Take out the index cards and brainstorm as a family to list all the thoughts, emotions, and feelings that might be used to describe how we feel when the Holy Ghost is present. Remember that negative emotions such as anger, hatred, and fear are not from the Spirit.

Talk about the situations you wrote on the papers. Working together, decide which types of feelings and promptings might be most appropriate for each situation, and place them with it.

Share a personal experience with the promptings of the Spirit, and help family members identify and describe their own experiences. Challenge them to try increasing their awareness of the many ways the Spirit communicates to them in different situations.

Activity

Experiment with making "telephones" out of tin cans or plastic cups. Observe that the best connections happen when the line is stretched tight. If you gently touch the string, you might even be able to feel the vibrations. Compare your experiences to the practice and firm commitment it takes to hear and follow the promptings of the Holy Ghost.

Treat

Warm Chocolate-Chip Cookies

1 cup butter-flavor shortening
1 cup brown sugar
1 cup sugar
2 eggs
1 ½ teaspoons vanilla
1 teaspoon salt
1 teaspoon baking soda
2 ¼ cups flour
2 cups chocolate chips

1. Cream the shortening, sugars, and eggs together.
2. Add the vanilla, salt and soda.
3. Gradually add the flour until completely mixed.
4. Gently fold in the chocolate chips.
5. Drop teaspoonfuls of dough onto a greased cookie sheet and bake for 8 to 10 minutes at 375°F.

Talk about why the smell and taste of the treat gives us feelings of warmth, security, and love. Remind the family that these are the feelings Heavenly Father wants us to have all the time. Providing this peace and comfort in ways we can understand is one important role of the Holy Ghost.

Additional Resources

James E. Faust, "How the Holy Ghost Helps You," *Friend*, Mar. 1990. https://www.lds.org/friend/1990/03/how-the-holy-ghost-helps-you?lang=eng

Margaret Lifferth, "Sharing Time: The Gift of the Holy Ghost," *Friend*, Aug. 2005. https://www.lds.org/friend/2005/08/sharing-time-the-gift-of-the-holy-ghost?lang=eng

"Understanding the Holy Ghost," *Friend*, Nov. 1974. https://www.lds.org/friend/1974/11/understanding-the-holy-ghost?lang=eng

"Preparation of Harold B. Lee: Boyhood Revelation," lds.org. http://www.lds.org/friend/online-activities/videos/prophets?lang=eng#harold-b-lee

Joseph Smith

Scripture

Joseph Smith—History 1:8, 10

Song

"A Young Man Prepared," *Children's Songbook*, 166

Preparation

Write the following on 11 index cards, one on each card: *typhoid fever, no more crutches, begins looking for true Church, First Vision, Moroni's first visit, gets married, receives gold plates, Book of Mormon is printed, Church is established, published Articles of Faith, martyrdom.* Shuffle the cards.

Lesson

Send the family members on a treasure hunt through the house to find things with each of the following numbers on them: 8, 11, 12, 14, 17, 22 (needed twice), 25 (needed twice), 38, and 39. If a certain number can't be found, they should find a creative way to represent that number. When all the numbers have been gathered, lay them out in order on a table or open floor space.

Hand the family your stack of index cards and explain that each one contains an event from the life of Joseph Smith. Family members will try to match the event with the number representing Joseph's age when that event occurred.

Joseph Smith was born on December 23, 1805. He, and the rest of his family, developed typhoid fever when he was eight years old. This infection resulted in the operation on his leg, the story of which is well known in the Church. For three years after the operation, Joseph couldn't walk without crutches, and he had a limp for the rest of his life. His interest in religion and his serious study of the scriptures in order to find the true Church of Jesus Christ began at approximately age 12, leading to the First Vision at 14. The Angel Moroni visited to tell him about the gold plates when Joseph was 17. He married Emma Hale when he was 22, and he obtained the gold plates later that same year. The Book of Mormon was published just prior to the official organization of the Church when Joseph was 25 years old. The Articles of Faith were published when he was 38, followed by his death at age 39.

Place the events in the correct order and talk about how they shaped Joseph's life and how he responded to the challenges they presented.

Discuss how blessed we are because Joseph Smith was willing to learn about the gospel, pray about his questions, and follow through with each piece of knowledge he received. His calling didn't make him less human or less prone to trials, but his righteous choices blessed many lives. Challenge family members to find ways to be more like Joseph in their cheerful attitude, integrity, and willingness to stand by their beliefs.

Activity

Have a stick pull. Use a long stick, a broom pole, or another pole that is at least four feet long. Have two family members sit down, facing each other with their knees bent and feet touching. They should grab the pole with their hands close together in the middle of the pole or stick. On the count of three, both people pull back on the poll. The first one to unseat his or her opponent wins.

Treat

Jonnycakes

1 cup cornmeal
¾ teaspoon salt

1 cup water

½ cup milk

1. Combine the salt and cornmeal in a mixing bowl and set aside.
2. Bring the water to a rolling boil on the stove.
3. Mix the water into the cornmeal, stirring constantly. When they are completely mixed, add the milk.
4. Drop the batter onto a hot, greased griddle and fry it like you would a pancake.
5. Serve warm with butter and honey or maple syrup.

Additional Resources

"Joseph Smith Seeks Wisdom in the Bible," lds.org. http://www.lds.org/friend/online-activities/activities/puzzles/joseph-smith-seeks-wisdom-in-the-bible?lang=eng

May Carter, "A Prophet is Born," *Friend*, Dec. 2012. http://media.ldscdn.org/pdf/magazines/friend-december-2012/2012-12-16-a-prophet-is-born-eng.pdf

Richard Lloyd Anderson, "The Early Preparation of the Prophet Joseph Smith," *Ensign*, Dec. 2005. http://www.lds.org/ensign/print/2005/12/the-early-preparation-of-the-prophet-joseph-smith?lang=eng&clang=eng

Sally Johnson Odekirk, "A Watch, Some Buttons, and Joseph's Cloak," *Ensign*, July 2008. https://www.lds.org/ensign/2008/07/a-watch-some-buttons-and-josephs-cloak?lang=eng

"Doctrine and Covenants, Chapter 1: Joseph Smith and His Family (1805–1820)," *Friend* videos, lds.org. http://www.lds.org/friend/online-activities/videos/scripture-stories/doctrine-and-covenants?lang=eng#1-joseph-smith-and-his-family-1805-1820

The Restoration of the Church

Scripture

Joseph Smith—History 1:14, 17

Song

"The Sacred Grove," *Children's Songbook*, 87

Preparation

Remove a handful of pieces from a 250-to-500-piece puzzle. Make sure you have a clear workspace big enough to work on the puzzle.

Lesson

Without showing the box, give the family the puzzle pieces you removed and ask them to put the puzzle together. When they are unable to, ask them why. Can they make a guess at what the puzzle picture shows from just the few pieces they have?

Explain the difference between the church that Jesus Christ established and those that began to appear after His death. When Christ was on the earth He gave His apostles specific instructions about what His Church should be like. Satan didn't want them to follow these instructions. Since most people could not read at that time, they had to count on their own memory to help them continue to do what was right. When questions came up, Christ was not there with the right answers, and within a number of years the apostles died as well. Local leaders of the Church struggled to do what they thought the Lord would want. Some people created different rules so they could become popular and rich by teaching what other people wanted to hear. Eventually the gospel of Jesus Christ had changed so much that the teachings and the priesthood became lost. There were still pieces left and some people were trying the best they could, but no one had the complete puzzle, or knew what it was supposed to look like any more.

Jesus Christ restored His Church through the Prophet Joseph Smith. To restore something means to bring it back or make it new again. Tell the story of the First Vision, paying special attention to the presence of the Spirit as you do so.

Explain that in the Restoration, Jesus Christ organized His Church once again here on the earth. He leads the Church through prophets and apostles. The Restoration also means that we have the fulness of the gospel of Jesus Christ. The gospel is made up of His teachings and commandments; ordinances like baptism, the sacrament, and temple marriage; and many other important things. Because we have the fulness of the gospel, we can understand the purposes of our lives and be happy. Express your gratitude for the blessing of knowing what Heavenly Father wants us to do.

Discuss some of the gospel truths we now have because of Joseph Smith's role in the Restoration, and how our lives might be different without this knowledge. Explain that we can know the Church is true by following its teachings and paying attention to the feelings we have when we learn about the gospel.

As each new topic is brought up, add a few more puzzle pieces to those available to the family. Finally, show the box and let the family see what the completed puzzle is supposed to look like. Explain that it is still our personal responsibility to understand what the pieces of the puzzle are and how they fit, but we can know what the end result and reward for our efforts will be. The gospel of Jesus Christ is much the same. Because of Joseph Smith we have the restored Church and the fulness of the gospel. We know the answers to life's most important questions, and we know what we need to do to become like Jesus and return to live with Him and Heavenly Father. But it is still up to each of us to learn, to understand, and to fit each of those pieces into our hearts and lives. As we learn and grow in the gospel, we gain access to more and more tools, or puzzle pieces, that we need to build a happy life and live up to Heavenly Father's vision for us. Express gratitude for Joseph Smith's role in giving us access to a complete puzzle, so that we can be happy now and in eternity.

Activity

Work together to complete the puzzle used in your lesson.

Treat

Baby Trees Bathed in Golden Light

> broccoli tops
> 1 can of Campbell's cheddar cheese soup,
>   or 1 jar of Tostitos Salsa con Queso
> ½ cup milk

1. Lightly steam the broccoli tops.
2. In a separate pan, combine the cheese sauce and milk. Warm over medium heat.
3. Pour the sauce over the broccoli prior to serving.

Additional Resources

"Preparation of Joseph Smith: The First Vision," Prophet Videos, lds.org. http://www.lds.org/friend/online-activities/videos/prophets?lang=eng#joseph-smith

"Special Witness: Elder Christofferson," lds.org. http://www.lds.org/media-library/video/2011-04-26-special-witness-elder-christofferson?lang=eng

Amie Jane Leavitt, "Partial Pictures," *Friend,* Aug. 2010. http://www.lds.org/bc/content/ldsorg/children/resources/topics/joseph-smith/Partial-Pictures-2010-08-friend.pdf?lang=eng

The Book of Mormon

Scripture
Joseph Smith—History 1:59

Song
"An Angel Came to Joseph Smith," *Children's Songbook*, 86

Preparation
Take some time to make a mental list of anything in your home that might be used as dress-up materials. Have a Book of Mormon available for use during the lesson.

Lesson
Warn family members prior to family home evening that it is masquerade night. They are to come to FHE dressed as their favorite character from the Book of Mormon. Help them with costume ideas as needed.

Begin the lesson with a general discussion of what the Book of Mormon is, where it came from, and why it is important. Then, let each family member introduce himself or herself as a favorite character from the book, and explain why that particular person or story is important to him or her.

When everyone has shared, bear your own testimony of the importance and truthfulness of the Book of Mormon. Show the family the title page of the Book of Mormon and discuss why this book of scripture is another testament of Jesus Christ. We read and study the Book of Mormon as a way to draw closer to Jesus Christ, just as we do when reading the Bible. Discuss some of the many different names used for Jesus Christ in the scriptures. Write them down so the children can recognize how the words are spelled and how they look.

Activity

Play a game called finding Jesus. Give each person a Book of Mormon and a colored pencil. Have each person open randomly to a page in the book. They are to find and color each reference to Christ on their chosen page.

Treat

Golden Plates

Graham crackers
Lemon icing

1. Cover graham crackers with lemon icing.
2. Write favorite scripture references in the icing with toothpicks.

Additional Resources

Diane L. Mangum, "The Book of Mormon Teaches of Jesus Christ," *Friend*, Jan. 2012. http://media.ldscdn.org/pdf/lds-magazines/friend-january-2012/2012-01-11-the-book-of-mormon-teaches-of-jesus-christ-eng.pdf

"Coming Forth of the Book of Mormon," *Friend*, Sept. 2004. http://www.lds.org/friend/2004/09/coming-forth-of-the-book-of-mormon?lang=eng

Julie T. Rabe, "I Will Read the Book of Mormon," *Friend*, Jan. 2008. http://www.lds.org/bc/content/ldsorg/children/resources/topics/book-of-mormon/I-Will-Read-the-Book-of-Mormon-FR_2008_01.pdf?lang=eng

"Mormon Messages: A Book with a Promise," lds.org. http://www.lds.org/media-library/video/mormon-messages/mormon-messages-2009?lang=eng#2009-03-11-a-book-with-a-promise

The Priesthood

Scripture

Doctrine and Covenants 20:60

Song

"The Priesthood Is Restored," *Children's Songbook*, 89

Preparation

Find a special family heirloom, or a story such as "Grandfather's Gold Watch" by Louise Garff Hubbard.

Lesson

Begin by sharing your heirloom or reading the story. Talk about the value of items that have been handed down from people we love. How do we care for such things?

When someone gives us a gift, it is usually because the person loves us and feels the gift will help make us happy. We show our thanks by taking care of the gift. Ask the family to sit in a circle and gently pass around your book or heirloom. Would it have been appropriate for someone to simply toss the item into the circle and let the other family members scramble to try to save it? What if one family member simply decided it was his or her turn to hold the object and tried to grab it away? What if someone decided he or she wanted to create a new special object? Could they say that a potato held the same value as the original treasure?

The priesthood is a very special gift from Heavenly Father. It is His power on earth. It is to be handled with respect and dignity and passed from one worthy man to another through sacred blessings called ordinations. When a man receives this gift and is worthy of it, he can act in Heavenly Father's name. If we are sick, the priesthood holder can lay his hands on our head to give us a blessing so we will get better or just feel God's comfort.

Discuss other times and ways the priesthood can be used. Why is it important for the person baptizing us to hold this priesthood?

Conclude by sharing a time when the priesthood has blessed your life personally. Challenge each family member to find one way he or she can better honor the priesthood during the coming week.

Activity

Play priesthood, priesthood, who's got the priesthood? (in the manner of button, button, who's got the button?). Have the family sit in a circle with their hands cupped closed in front of them. Place a small key inside your own cupped hands and quietly go around to each person, pretending to drop the key into their hands. Choose one family member to receive the key. The others must guess who holds the "priesthood keys." The child holding the key begins the next round of play.

Treat

John the Baptist's Warm Milk and Honey

4 cups milk
4 teaspoons honey
1 teaspoon vanilla extract

1. Warm the milk over medium-low heat until it is very hot and begins to foam slightly.
2. Remove from heat and stir in honey and vanilla.
3. Serve with Keebler Grasshopper cookies.

Additional Resources

Kimberly Webb, "Heaven's Power," *Friend,* May 2005.
http://www.lds.org/bc/content/ldsorg/children/
resources/topics/priesthood/Heavens-Power-2005-05-
friend.pdf?lang=eng

Gordon B. Hinckley, "The Restoration of the Priesthood,"
Friend, May 2003. http://www.lds.org/bc/content/ldsorg/
children/resources/topics/priesthood/The-Restoration-of-
the-Priesthood-2003-05-friend.pdf?lang=eng

"Chapter 37: Priesthood Leaders (February—March
1835)," Doctrine and Covenants Stories, lds.org.
http://www.lds.org/media-library/video/2010-06-
38-chapter-37-priesthood-leaders-february-march-
1835?category=doctrine-and-covenants/doctrine-and-
covenants-stories&&lang=eng

"Blessings of the Priesthood," Mormon Messages, lds.org.
http://www.lds.org/media-library/video/2009-05-20-
blessings-of-the-priesthood?category=mormon-messages/
mormon-messages-2009&&lang=eng

A Living Prophet

Scripture

Amos 3:7

Song

"Latter-day Prophets," *Children's Songbook*, 134

Lesson

Name a few of the prophets talked about in the scriptures. Ask your family to identify those prophets' stories and how the stories are alike. If it was important for people who lived long ago to have prophets to lead and guide them, is it important for us to have a prophet today?

Ask family members if they have ever been inside a maze. How did the experience feel? Was it easy to find your way through to your goal? Would it have been easier or harder to go through with a friend? What if there was someone who could see the entire maze from a different perspective and was willing to guide you through?

The gospel of Jesus Christ remains the same whether it is the time of Adam, Noah, Nephi, Paul, or right now. A key feature of the true Church of Jesus Christ is a leader who bears the priesthood of God and has been called to lead and guide His Church. Ask the family to name the current President of the Church and tell you anything they can about him. Can any other modern prophets be named? Can family members recall any stories they have heard about these men?

Explain that while all members of the First Presidency and the Quorum of the Twelve Apostles are prophets, seers, and revelators, the President of the Church, who is the senior apostle, is usually known as "the prophet." He receives revelation from Jesus Christ for all of God's children and leads and directs the Church in righteousness. We pray for the prophet, sustain him, and look to him to guide us through life's mazes with a view that is better than our own.

Challenge each family member to research one prophet and bring a story from his life to the next family home evening. Also challenge family members to sustain the counselors in the First Presidency and the members of the Quorum of the Twelve Apostles. Encourage family members to learn about the purpose of prophets and apostles.

Activity

Play a game of guess the prophet. Use the images of the prophets found on lds.org (http://www.lds.org/media-library/images/gospel-art/latter-day-prophets?lang=eng) to create two sets of cards of the latter-day prophets.

One family member draws a prophet out of one stack of cards and holds it so only he or she can see it. The rest of the family spreads out the other deck of cards and begins asking yes or no questions about the picture, e.g., "Does your prophet have a beard," or "Does your prophet wear glasses?" Depending on how the person answers who is holding the prophet card, eliminate cards until you think you know which prophet has been chosen.

Treat

Saltwater Taffy

2 cups sugar

1 cup light corn syrup

1 cup water

1 ½ teaspoons salt

2 teaspoons butter

¼ teaspoon flavoring of choice

5 to 7 drops of food coloring

1. Combine the sugar, corn syrup, water, and salt. Cook over medium heat, stirring constantly, until the mixture reaches approximately 250°F (hard-ball stage).
2. Remove from heat and stir in butter, flavor, and coloring.
3. Pour into a well-buttered pan and let cool for about 20 minutes.
4. When the candy is easy to handle, butter your hands and pull the candy until the sheen dulls and it becomes too hard to pull.
5. Cut into bite-size pieces and wrap in wax paper or plastic wrap.

Additional Resources

M. Russell Ballard, "Special Witness: Our Living Prophet," *Friend,* May 2003. http://www.lds.org/friend/2003/05/special-witness-our-living-prophet?lang=eng

Neil L. Andersen, "Why Are Prophets important?" *Friend,* Mar. 2012. http://media.ldscdn.org/pdf/lds-magazines/friend-march-2012/2012-03-06-why-are-prophets-important-eng.pdf

"Follow the Prophet," *Friend,* May 2013. http://media.ldscdn.org/pdf/magazines/friend-may-2013/2013-05-22-following-the-prophet-eng.pdf

"We Need Living Prophets," lds.org. http://www.lds.org/media-library/video/2012-04-15-we-need-living-prophets?lang=eng

"Latter-day Prophets," lds.org. http://www.lds.org/friend/online-activities/activities/matching/latter-day-prophets?lang=eng

Prayer

Scripture
Mark 11:24

Song
"A Child's Prayer," *Children's Songbook*, 12

Preparation
Fill a small basket with items that make a variety of noises, such as sandpaper, jingle bell, bubble wrap, and keys.

Lesson
After singing the opening song, review the lyrics with your family and ask them what they think of when they sing the words, or what types of feelings they bring. Emphasize the truthfulness of the song's message, and help family members understand that this promise is for every child of God. It does not say that Heavenly Father only listens to moms, dads, bishops, or prophets. He cares about and wants to talk with all of His children, and He always listens. The best thing we can do is talk to Him in prayer and listen for His answers.

Ask each family member to relate a favorite scripture story about prayer. Discuss the similarities and difference between the stories. For instance, which circumstances or places were similar? Did Heavenly Father always answer the prayer? Did He always give the same answer or answer in the same way? Next, ask your family to think of similar situations they might find themselves in. Identify specific times and ways to pray. Remind everyone that God is always ready to listen whenever we need Him.

Tell family members to close their eyes while you use the items you prepared to make sounds. Ask your family to identify what kind of item made each sound. Talk about what made it easier or harder to recognize a sound (how quiet the room was, how long the noise lasted, how loud or soft it was, how familiar family members were with the given noise, etc.). Remind the family that one of the greatest blessings of prayer is the chance we give Heavenly Father to talk with us as well, but we have to be willing to listen. The ways He can communicate are just as different as the sounds the family members heard or the methods they discussed in their scripture stories. It is up to each of us to learn how to hear or feel Heavenly Father's influence. Promise the family that as they practice offering sincere prayers and listening for answers, they will begin to recognize the ways He communicates with them. This method may be different for each family member because Heavenly Father knows which ways each person can hear and learn from Him best.

Tell family members how important it is to learn to hear Heavenly Father, just as they learned to listen in the game. Learning to listen better might include being quiet before you pray, taking time to think about what you want to say, finding a special and private place to pray, praying out loud when you can, using sacred names when referring to Heavenly Father in prayer, taking time to think about what you have been praying for before ending your prayer, and reading your scriptures and attending Church meetings where Heavenly can use other ways to answer your questions. Remind the family that the more they practice praying and listening, the easier it will be to know Heavenly Father is listening and to hear what He wants to say to us in return.

Activity

Continue with the sound-guessing game from the lesson. Let each family member collect one mystery object for everyone else to guess. Challenge each person to work on listening for Heavenly Father's answers to prayers.

Treat

Make "easy elephant ears." Fry six-inch flour tortillas in oil and top them with cinnamon and sugar, powdered sugar, or anything else that sounds yummy.

Additional Resources

Ezra Taft Benson, "Prayer," *Ensign*, May 1977. http://www.lds.org/ensign/1977/05/prayer?lang=eng

"Did You Think to Pray?" *Friend*, Sept. 2008. http://www.lds.org/friend/2008/09/did-you-think-to-pray?lang=eng

April Stott, "I Can Pray to Heavenly Father, and He Will Hear and Answer My Prayer," *Liahona*, Sept. 2008. http://www.lds.org/liahona/2008/09/coloring-page?lang=eng

Tadd R. Peterson, "Prayer," *Liahona*, Jan. 2005. http://www.lds.org/liahona/2005/01/prayer?lang=eng

Testimony

Scripture

Moroni 10:4–5

Song

"Search, Ponder, and Pray," *Children's Songbook,* 109

Preparation

Gather a sheet of paper and pen or pencil for each member of the family. You will also need a potted plant, yarn or thin ribbon, and scissors.

Lesson

Ask family members why one sacrament meeting per month is dedicated to bearing testimony. Explain that a testimony is the foundation of our beliefs and membership in Christ's true Church.

Discuss the following questions: Why is it important to have a testimony of Jesus Christ and His Church? How do we get a testimony? Does a testimony ever grow or change? How does having a testimony of Jesus Christ change how we live our lives?

Show your potted plant. Talk about the ways you can nurture it and help it grow. What would happen if you never watered the plant and didn't give it enough sunlight? What happens to a testimony when it isn't nurtured? Having a healthy plant requires a bit of work on our part. Keeping a testimony strong and growing also requires work and dedication.

Have the family help each other trace both of their hands on a sheet of paper. Discuss ways to strengthen testimony. As each point is explained and discussed, decide on a short phrase or picture that can be written on each finger of the hand sketches, to represent the topic. Try to fill each finger with a way to strengthen testimonies.

Share your own testimony with your family. Conclude family home evening with a challenge for each person to find one way to strengthen his or her testimony in the coming weeks. Cut out the hands made by your family and have them gently tie a "reminder ribbon" around the finger that best represents what they are going to work on. Encourage each person to put his or her hand drawing in a place where he or she can see it every day, as a reminder to consistently nurture and build testimony.

Activity

Hold a family testimony meeting. Pay special attention to the feelings in the room, and help the children realize that these feelings indicate the presence of the Holy Ghost and are part of a testimony.

Treat

Seeds of Testimony

1 egg white
¾ cup sugar
¾ teaspoon cinnamon
dash salt
½ teaspoon vanilla
4 cups raw, unsalted sunflower seeds

1. Mix egg whites, sugar, cinnamon, salt, and vanilla together.
2. Stir in the sunflower seeds until they are evenly coated.
3. Spread on a cookie sheet and bake for 10 minutes at 300°F.
4. Remove the cookie sheet from the oven and stir the seeds, then return to the oven for an additional 5 to 8 minutes. Cool seeds before serving.

Additional Resources

"Matt and Mandy: A Testimony," lds.org. http://www.lds.org/friend/online-activities/videos/matt-mandy?lang=eng#a-testimony

Robert D. Hales, "How can I get a Testimony?" *Friend,* Jan. 2013. http://media.ldscdn.org/pdf/magazines/friend-january-2013/2013-01-18-how-can-i-get-a-testimony-eng.pdf

Joshua J. Perkey, "Thomas's Testimony," *Friend,* July 2012. http://media.ldscdn.org/pdf/magazines/friend-july-2012/2012-07-07-thomass-testimony-eng.pdf

"A Growing Testimony," *Friend,* July 2012. http://media.ldscdn.org/pdf/magazines/friend-july-2012/2012-07-08-a-growing-testimony-eng.pdf

"Testimony Glove," *Friend,* Oct. 2008. https://www.lds.org/friend/2008/10/testimony-glove?lang=eng

The Plan of Salvation

Scripture

Mosiah 2:41

Song

"I Will Follow God's Plan," *Children's Songbook*, 164

Preparation

Collect a few items that people would take on vacation, such as a map, camera, and guidebook.

Lesson

Begin by talking to your family about a memorable trip you have taken together. What was the purpose of the trip? How did you prepare? Did everything always go the way you planned? How did it feel to come home again?

Explain that people go on trips and vacations for many different reasons. They could be going to visit someone, looking for a place to relax, or just heading off to do something fun. They plan to return home when the vacation is over. They use various tools to help get where they are going and to have a good time on the trip. They might use their car or a plane, a map, suggestions on where to go, money for things they need, etc.

Now, have family members imagine they are once again in the premortal life, preparing for their trip to earth, and the time they would spend here. How do the two scenarios compare? What did we do to prepare before we left Heavenly Father's presence and came to earth? Why were we going? Did we look forward to our time on earth, or dread it? What tools were in place for us to use while we were away from home? What did we need to find and do while we were here, in order to return home to Heavenly Father again?

Explain that we know the answers to many of these questions because we have the gospel of Jesus Christ. There are many people on earth who are unable to answer three very important questions: Where did we come from? Why are we here? Where do we go after we die?

How would it feel to find yourself away from home with no idea why you were there or what you needed to do to get back again?

Discuss the ways we can find joy in our time away from heaven. Talk about what to do when we get lost or if our journey gets rough. What kind of memories do we want to return home with?

Remind your family that while our time on earth is of great importance in our eternal progression, what makes it good is the choices and opportunities we have along the way. Not everyone experiences the same trip, and even if we are headed for the same place, what we see and do along the way is unique to each of us. We use the tools Heavenly Father has given us and speak with Him often to help us decide the best ways to find joy in life. When we remember to do these things, our time away from Him can be an amazing experience that will help us grow, gain important knowledge, and make beautiful memories to take home with us.

Activity

Play the suitcase game. Each player repeats a phrase such as "When I return to live with Heavenly Father, in my suitcase I will bring . . ." Then the person names an item of spiritual or eternal value that begins with either a letter of the alphabet (start with *A* and go through the alphabet), or the first letter in the person's name. Each subsequent player must repeat the items carried back to Heavenly Father by the players who have gone before him or her, before adding his or her own idea.

Treat

Three-Degrees-of-Glory Dessert

3.4-ounce package instant chocolate pudding, prepared
1 package of Nutter Butter® cookies, broken into bite-size
    pieces
3.4-ounce package instant vanilla pudding, prepared
1 eight-ounce container whipped topping

Layer the ingredients in a glass bowl in this order:
1. Chocolate pudding (outer darkness)
2. Cookie pieces (telestial kingdom)
3. Vanilla pudding (terrestrial kingdom)
4. Whipped topping (celestial kingdom)

Additional Resources

"Introduction: Our Heavenly Father's Plan," New Testament
    Stories, lds.org. http://www.lds.org/media-library/video/
    new-testament/new-testament-stories?lang=eng#2010-11-
    01-introduction-our-heavenly-fathers-plan

Thomas S. Monson, "The Race of Life," *Ensign,* May 2012.
    http://www.lds.org/media-library/video/2012-04-0170-
    the-race-of-life?lang=eng

Ann Jamison, "Sharing Time: On the Right Path," *Friend,*
    Jan. 2000. http://www.lds.org/friend/2000/01/sharing-
    time-on-the-right-path?lang=eng

Dallin H. Oaks, "The Great Plan of Happiness," *Friend,*
    Apr. 1995. http://www.lds.org/friend/1995/04/the-great-
    plan-of-happiness?lang=eng

Service

Scripture

Alma 37:6–7

Song

"Give, Said the Little Stream," *Children's Songbook,* 236

Preparation

Obtain a picture of Jesus teaching in the temple as a child (see *Gospel Art Book,* 34).

Lesson

Show your family the picture of Jesus in the temple and have them help you tell the story it portrays.

Ask the family how they feel about Jesus' actions in this story. Was He doing something good? Was everything about the story good? Explain that He knew He had a very important service to give in the temple. However, His parents thought He was with other family members in their group as they left Jerusalem to travel back to their home in Nazareth, and two days into the journey Mary and Joseph realized He was missing. They thought He was lost, but He was safe, teaching the priests in the temple, and answering their questions. From the time He was a child, Jesus placed Himself in a position to help and teach others. This is the way He lived His entire life. Others around Him might not have understood why He went where He went or why He did what He did. But Jesus always went where He could do the most good.

Read Luke 9:24 as a family and discuss the message of the verse. Explain that like Jesus, we can choose to serve others. While it is not appropriate to be away without telling an adult where you are, it is always appropriate to love and serve others. Discuss the good we can do when we reach out to others. Explain that no matter who we are, we have opportunities and choices, and each of us brings our own unique gifts and talents to those situations. The challenge is to find ways to use our gifts to serve others.

Share times when, within your own family, you have given a unique service or been the recipient of a thoughtful gesture. Challenge family members to find ways to get lost in service and find joy in it.

Brainstorm service ideas and create a "What can I do?" list for your family. Write down as many different life challenges as you can think of, and for each one add several things that can be done to help a person in that situation. Designate a spot in your home for the list where everyone can refer to it when they see someone in need but don't know how to help.

Consider ending each day with the question "What have I done for someone today?"

Activity

Play hide-and-seek with a service twist. Each family member chooses a hiding spot that represents a way he or she likes to serve others. (One might hide in the pantry where her baking supplies are, because she likes to cook for others; another might hide under the piano because he enjoys playing for Church meetings, etc.) When the person who is "it" finds someone else, the found person runs for home base. "It" must call out what he or she thinks the other person's chosen service was before that person reaches home base, in order to "catch" the runner in the act.

Treat

Sweetness Sprinkled with Love

6 ounces white chocolate
6 tablespoons butter

1/3 cup water

3.4-ounce package instant vanilla pudding

3 cups powdered sugar

¼ cup rainbow sprinkles

1. Grease an 8-inch pan, or line it with foil.
2. Heat chocolate, butter, and water in the microwave until butter is completely melted. Stir until mixture is smooth.
3. Add the pudding mix and stir until well blended. Gradually add the powdered sugar, mixing thoroughly after each addition. Gently fold in the candy sprinkles.
4. Press the fudge into the prepared pan, top with additional sprinkles, and refrigerate for two hours.
5. Cut fudge into small pieces and share with a friend or neighbor who needs to know he or she is loved.

Additional Resources

Thomas S. Monson, "What Have I Done for Someone Today?" *Ensign*, Nov. 2009. http://www.lds.org/ensign/2009/11/what-have-i-done-for-someone-today?lang=eng

M. Russell Ballard, "Finding Joy through Loving Service," *Ensign*, May 2011. http://www.lds.org/ensign/2011/05/finding-joy-through-loving-service?lang=eng

Matt and Mandy, "365 Days of Service," *Friend*, Jan. 2010. http://www.lds.org/friend/online-activities/videos/matt-mandy?lang=eng#365-days-of-service

"The Coat," *Friend*, Mar. 2012. http://www.lds.org/media-library/video/topics/service?lang=eng#2011-12-001-the-coat

"A Playground for Carly," lds.org. http://www.lds.org/friend/online-activities/videos/other?lang=eng#a-playground-for-carly

Obedience

Scripture

Doctrine and Covenants 76:5

Song

"Nephi's Courage," *Children's Songbook*, 120

Preparation

Prayerfully read and review the story of Nehemiah and the protection of Jerusalem (see Nehemiah 1 through 6). A similar message can be found in Alma 47.

Lesson

Invite an older child or adult family member to come forward and hold his or her arms out to the side. Challenge the person to keep doing this even when you try to force his or her arms down. Apply gentle pressure and talk about the resistance you feel. Next, quietly divert the person's attention by talking about something else, rubbing his or her back, or doing another small action that will cause the person to lose focus. Then, swiftly push down on one of his or her arms, causing it to drop.

Practice this with other members of the family. Talk about the difference between the two challenges. During the first moments of the challenge, the person with his or her arms out is expecting you to apply pressure to his or her arms. The person is prepared and able to withstand the pressure you put on his or her arms. What happens when he or she is distracted? The person may still exert some resistance, but his or her arm will drop much more readily.

Next, have the family prepare a short list of the things they think are most important in their lives. These might include their family, the gospel, school studies, etc. Then, they should list everything they can remember about what they did that day. How many of their activities that day were directly related to the things they said mattered most? Which things sneaked into their day that took time or attention away from what they wanted or needed to be doing?

Share the story of Nehemiah. Discuss as a family why it is so important to keep our focus on the gospel. Ask, "How can Satan distract us?" and "What defenses do we have against his tactics?" As a family, what adjustments can you make to your daily lives that will help build your family defenses? What individuals goals can you set?

Now that your family is aware of the trick you used to make someone drop his or her arms, pair up and see how much effort it takes to get those arms back down to each person's side. Remind the family that we have more strength and power than Satan, unless we give him power over us. Explain that he obtains power by distracting us and taking our thoughts away from Heavenly Father. As the scriptures tell us, "No man can serve two masters" (3 Nephi 13:24).

Encourage family members to keep their arms firm and not allow themselves to be distracted from those things that matter most.

Activity

Play a game of red rover. Divide the family into two teams. Go outdoors so you have plenty of running space. Each team forms a line by holding hands or locking arms. The teams take turns calling someone from the opposing team to come over by saying, "Red rover, red rover, send [name of player on opposite team] right over." That person runs toward the opposite line and tries to break through their joined hands. If the person can't break through, he or she has to join that team's line. If the person does break through, he or she can choose an opposing player to go back with him or her to the other side. Play continues until all the family members end up on one side.

Treat

Monkey-Bread Wall for Nehemiah's Jerusalem

3 cans refrigerated biscuit dough
1 cup sugar
2 teaspoons cinnamon
½ cup margarine

1. Combine the cinnamon and sugar in a small bowl. Melt the butter in another bowl.
2. Cut the biscuits in half with kitchen scissors.
3. Roll each piece of biscuit in the butter, then in the cinnamon and sugar.
4. Stack the coated pieces in and around a greased Bundt pan.
5. Bake the biscuit formation for 35 minutes at 350°F.
6. Let the bread cool slightly, then turn it out onto a plate. The individual pieces of dough will pull apart from each other.

Additional Resources

Dieter F. Uchtdorf, "We Are Doing a Great Work and Cannot Come Down," *Friend,* May 2009. http://www.lds.org/ensign/2009/05/we-are-doing-a-great-work-and-cannot-come-down?lang=eng

Darlene Young, "Andy's Choice," *Friend,* May 2008. http://www.lds.org/bc/content/ldsorg/children/resources/topics/obedience/Andys-Choice-2008-05-friend.pdf?lang=eng

Diane Nichols, "Obedience Brings Blessings," *Friend,* May 2001. http://www.lds.org/bc/content/ldsorg/children/resources/topics/obedience/Obedience-Brings-Blessings-2001-05-friend.pdf?lang=eng

Heather Brinkerhoff, "CTR Pretzels," *Friend,* Jan. 2012. http://media.ldscdn.org/pdf/lds-magazines/friend-january-2012/2012-01-14-ctr-pretzels-eng.pdf

Choices and Consequences

Scripture

2 Timothy 1:7

Song

"Choose the Right Way," *Children's Songbook*, 160

Preparation

Bring crayons and sheets of paper.

Lesson

Pass out the paper and crayons and ask your family to draw a picture of a family rule and why it keeps them safe. Ideas might include not crossing the street without an adult, cooking only when supervised, or not talking to strangers. Share the pictures and discuss each of the rules, and the consequences that might come from breaking it. Acknowledge that even though there are times when breaking a rule doesn't seem to cause any harm (we don't always get run over by a car if we don't use a crosswalk to cross the street), the potential danger is still there. Ignoring the rule once may lead us to ignore it more often until something bad happens.

Next, discuss some of the commandments and the reasons the Lord gave them. How do they keep us safe? What kinds of protection do they offer? Remind the children that consequences are not always obvious or severely damaging, but each time we break a commandment we lose the companionship of the Holy Ghost and open doorways to problems that could have been easily avoided.

Explain and discuss the concept of accountability and why eight years is the age of accountability.

Place a kernel of popping corn or a small pebble in each person's shoe and go on a short walk. Talk about the different choices each person had regarding the irritant—finding a more comfortable spot for it, ignoring it, removing it, etc. Discuss the consequences of each choice. Remind the children that no one else can be responsible for taking the pebble out of their shoe. Each person chooses for himself or herself how to deal with it, based on that person's knowledge and experience. For instance, a daughter may ask for help and follow others' examples, but if her brother chooses to remove his own pebble and she does not remove hers, she will still feel discomfort.

We make similar choices every day based on the rules and guidelines in our home, the commandments of God, and the laws in the area where we live. Others may not always see the choices we have to make, but whether or not a good or bad choice is witnessed by someone else does not change the consequences and our accountability for the choice.

Activity

Play a game of hands down. Label each one of a large stack of index cards with the word *good*. Label a smaller stack of cards *bad*. Shuffle the cards together. Hold the stack of cards upside down and quickly flip them over one at a time. If a good card is turned over, the first person to slap his or her hand down over it gets the card. If someone accidentally slaps a bad card, he or she must repent and forfeit one good card to be shuffled back into the pile. When all the cards are turned, the person who collected the highest number of *good* cards is the winner.

Treat

Crepes

1 cup flour
2 eggs

½ cup milk

½ cup water

¼ teaspoon salt

2 tablespoons melted butter

1. Whip eggs and flour together. Slowly add in the water and milk until well combined. Add the salt and butter last.
2. Pour batter into a greased frying pan until the batter barely covers the surface. Cook over medium heat until each side is brown, then remove from pan. Repeat until all batter has been used.
3. Serve crepes hot. Provide a wide variety of topping choices, including a few that would probably not be wise combinations.

Additional Resources

Thomas S. Monson, "May You Have Courage," *Ensign,* May 2009. http://www.lds.org/ensign/2009/05/may-you-have-courage?lang=eng

Sharing Time, "I Am Accountable for My Choices," *Friend,* Feb. 2000. http://www.lds.org/friend/2000/02/sharing-time-i-am-accountable-for-my-choices?lang=eng

Karen Ashton, "My Choices Have Consequences," *Friend,* Mar. 1997. http://www.lds.org/bc/content/ldsorg/children/resources/topics/choose-the-right/My-Choices-Have-Consequences-1997-03-friend.pdf?lang=eng

Repentance

Scripture

Alma 5:33

Song

"Repentance," *Children's Songbook,* 98

Preparation

Find a bandana or other cloth that can be used as a blindfold. You will also need sheets of paper and crayons.

Lesson

Begin by bringing two members of the family to the front of the room. Blindfold one of them, then instruct him or her to listen carefully. The other family member should silently move to another location in the room, then whisper the blindfolded person's name. That person must turn and point to where the voice came from. Raise the difficulty by having two or three family members call the person's name. The person must then discern the voice he or she is supposed to be listening for and point to the right family member.

Work together, using your scriptures, to create a working definition of sin. What is it? How does it affect our relationship with ourselves, others, and our Heavenly Father?

Read Alma 5:33 together. Discuss the concept of repentance, and how and why Jesus Christ would call to us and plead for us to willingly repent of our sins.

Remind the family that Heavenly Father does not gain pleasure from watching His children struggle, or from pointing out their sins. What He seeks is our willingness to put away things that keep us from being close to Him and feeling His love.

Discuss the places various members of the family like to go when they need to feel loved and safe. Why do these places bring comfort?

The Savior desires that we turn to Him when we are having a difficult time. Emphasize His interest in and understanding of the problems and pain we each face. He wants us to find our way back to Him so He can offer us love, comfort, and forgiveness. To repent is to single out His voice from all the others we might hear and turn toward Him, just as the family member turned toward the person calling his or her name in the opening activity.

What voices and obstacles can block our way when we try to repent and turn back to Christ? Discuss the influence of friends, media, personal expectations, and even loss of self-worth on an individual's ability to repent and return to God.

Make heart puzzles with construction paper. Draw large hearts, and inside each one, draw a picture of someone following the commandments. Cut the hearts into puzzle pieces and exchange them with other family members. Discuss the steps of repentance and how they can be used to find Jesus' comforting arms as you use tape or glue to put together the puzzles.

Activity

Play blind man's bluff. This version of tag requires an open area to play. The person who is "it" is blindfolded, and the other family members try to avoid being touched by him or her while staying within the established play area. Players can try to move as quietly as possible to avoid detection, or talk to and "taunt" the person who is "it," while still managing to avoid being touched. The first person caught becomes the next person to be blindfolded.

Treat

Make heart-shaped grilled cheese sandwiches. Remind the children of the warmth and goodness that come from giving our hearts and our obedience over to Heavenly Father and the healing power of the Atonement of Jesus Christ.

Additional Resources

Anne Bentley Waddoups, "Clean Again," *Friend*, Oct. 2006. http://www.lds.org/bc/content/ldsorg/children/resources/topics/repentance/Clean-Again-2006-10-friend.pdf?lang=eng

"Repentance and the Atonement," *Friend*, Mar. 2004. http://www.lds.org/liahona/2004/03/repentance-and-the-atonement?lang=eng

Darcie Jensen, "Learning from Mistakes," *Friend*, July 2012. http://www.lds.org/bc/content/shared/content/images/magazines/friend/2012/07/fr12jul34-learning-from-mistakes.pdf?lang=eng

Baptism

Scripture

Doctrine and Covenants 68:27

Song

"Baptism," *Children's Songbook,* 100

Preparation

Obtain a picture of Jesus Christ being baptized (see *Gospel Art Book,* 35).

Lesson

Play a simple game of follow-the-leader. Then, ask your family to name some of the people they should follow in real life. Answers might include a parent, teacher, the prophet, or another respected individual. Discuss the reasons these people are good examples, and the types of things they do that make someone want to follow them. Remind the family that of all the people they could want to follow and be like, Jesus Christ will always be our perfect example. We can look to Him no matter what kind of problems we face.

Tell the family that today you will discuss one important thing we do when we want to follow Jesus Christ. Read Matthew 3:13–15 together as a family. Show your picture and discuss the story of Jesus' baptism. Remind the family that one reason He was baptized was to show us what we need to do. Ask the family why baptism is necessary for all of Heavenly Father's children. Allow family members to share the thoughts and impressions that came to them as they followed Christ's example to be baptized.

Remind the family that at our baptism we promise Heavenly Father that we will follow Jesus Christ as our example in all things. We express our desire to be like Him and stand as a witness for Him no matter where we are.

Discuss the blessings that come from making the promises of baptism, which are called covenants. Being baptized and confirmed allows us to obtain the gift of the Holy Ghost and starts us on the pathway that leads back to Heavenly Father, where we can live with Him as an eternal family.

Choosing to be baptized is a great blessing to the person being baptized, but it is also a blessing to the person's family and others he or she associates with. Ask the family to share their thoughts on why this might be.

Share Mosiah 18:8—10 with the family. In these verses, Alma explains the baptismal covenant. Ask family members to identify the things we covenant to do when we are baptized, such as coming into the fold of God, bearing one another's burdens, mourning with those that mourn, and standing as a witness of God. Discuss ways you can follow these actions to help you become closer as a family. Remind each family member that when we are baptized we commit to do our best to be Christlike. We keep our baptismal covenants by obeying the commandments, strengthening our family, being an example to others, and helping people when they are in need. Following Christ in these ways allows the Holy Ghost to be in our home and with each family member.

Remind the family that when this challenge was extended to the people at the waters of Mormon, they clapped for joy because they knew making these covenants would bring them lasting happiness. Testify that keeping the covenants we make at baptism and listening to the promptings of the Spirit will bring great happiness to your family. Challenge each family member to watch for ways he or she can meet the challenges Alma gave in conjunction with baptism. Watch to see the difference it makes in the family.

Activity

Continue playing follow-the-leader.

Treat

Serve strawberries and white-chocolate fondue. While family members dip their strawberries in the fondue, talk about why we are baptized by immersion, the symbolism of this true doctrine, and the Atonement's ability to turn even our deepest sins into something pure and clean again (see Isaiah 1:18).

Additional Resources

Robert D. Hales, "Baptism," *Friend,* Jan. 2003. http://www.lds.org/bc/content/ldsorg/children/resources/topics/baptism/Baptism-2003-01-friend.pdf?lang=eng

Jose M. "My Decision to Be Baptized," *Liahona,* Apr. 2006. http://www.lds.org/bc/content/ldsorg/children/resources/topics/baptism/My-Decision-to-Be-Baptized-2006-04-Liahona.pdf?lang=eng

"When I am baptized, I make a covenant with God," *Friend,* June 2011. http://www.lds.org/bc/content/shared/content/images/magazines/friend/2011/06/fr11jun46-color.pdf?lang=eng

Covenants

Scripture

Alma 46:15

Song

"I Will Be Valiant," *Children's Songbook,* 162

Preparation

From a large ball of string or yarn, cut nine long pieces.

Lesson

Discuss the importance of our baptismal covenants. Clarify the meaning of *covenant* as needed.

Read Mosiah 18:8–10 together. Call attention to the three most important covenants made at baptism. These are becoming a member of the Church (come unto the fold and be called His people), serving God, and keeping His commandments. Each of these things will be represented by one strand of yarn.

The other items listed are important, but for the most part they fall under one of the three main covenants. For instance, bearing another's burden is serving God by serving one of His children, and standing as a witness of God no matter where we are is part of being a member of the true Church.

Take the three strands and braid them together as you discuss how these covenants work together, and ways they can be implemented in our lives. Moroni 6:4–9 can add to your discussion as needed.

Explain how you took something small to create something bigger and stronger than each strand could have been on its own.

This is the way covenants work. When we make and honor them faithfully, Heavenly Father blesses us in return. Use Mosiah 18:10 to talk about the blessings He promises us when we are baptized. Discuss the blessings that can come from listening to and following the Spirit.

Show the next three pieces of string and use 1 Corinthians 3:16–17 (morality and respecting our bodies), 3 Nephi 11:29 (avoiding contention), and 3 Nephi 18:17 (remembering Christ) to show ways we honor our baptismal covenants. Braid the pieces together while discussing other ways we can have the Spirit with us in our daily lives.

Return to 3 Nephi 18:17 and identify the way this verse gives us to remember Christ. Each week in sacrament meeting, as we reverently listen to the sacrament prayers and partake of the bread and water, we renew the covenants we made at baptism. The sacrament is a sacred ordinance that helps us repent of our sins and be forgiven, just like when we were baptized.

Read Doctrine and Covenants 20:77 and identify the last three promises made and renewed during the sacrament—taking Christ's name upon us, remembering Him, and keeping His commandments. These promises are represented by the remaining three strands of yarn. When we take the sacrament, we promise that we will continue to obey the Lord's commandments. If we keep our promise, He promises to forgive our sins and that we will have the Holy Ghost with us.

Now braid together the individual covenant braids you created. Explain that honoring these covenants and gifts keep us safe and strong in the gospel now, but also prepares us to make and keep the greater covenants of the temple. The more we make promises with our Heavenly Father and try to do what is right, the stronger our faith and testimony becomes.

End by bearing your own testimony, encouraging your family to work at keeping their covenants every day.

Activity

Make string mazes. Take turns using a ball of string to mark an obstacle course through the home or yard that other family members must follow (rewinding the ball as they go, as able). Reinforce the importance of keeping our covenants so we can stay on the path the Lord has laid out for us—the path that leads back home to Him.

Treat

Braided Breadsticks and Pizza Sauce

3 cans refrigerated biscuit dough
1 stick butter
Parmesan cheese
garlic powder
pizza sauce

1. Roll each biscuit into a long, thin rope. Braid three ropes, then pinch the ends together. Continue braiding the dough until all the biscuits have been used.
2. Place the braided breadsticks on a greased cookie sheet.
3. Melt the butter and generously brush it on the breadsticks. Sprinkle with garlic powder and Parmesan cheese.
4. Bake according to the biscuit package directions.
5. Serve the breadsticks with pizza sauce for dipping.

Additional Resources

Robert D. Hales, "Of His Kingdom," *Friend*, Oct. 2002. http://www.lds.org/bc/content/ldsorg/children/resources/topics/covenants/Of-His-Kingdom-2002-10-friend.pdf?lang=eng

Ann Jamison, "Sharing Time: A Sacred Promise," *Friend*, Mar. 2000. http://www.lds.org/liahona/2000/03/sharing-time-a-sacred-promise?lang=eng

Karen Ashton, "Baptism: My First Covenant," *Friend*, May
    1997. http://www.lds.org/bc/content/ldsorg/children/
    resources/topics/baptism/Baptism-My-First-Covenant-
    1997-05-friend.pdf?lang=eng
Diane L. Mangum, "Alma Baptizes," *Friend*, July 2012.
    http://media.ldscdn.org/pdf/magazines/friend-july-
    2012/2012-07-11-alma-baptizes-eng.pdf

The Sacrament

Scripture

Matthew 26:26–29

Song

"Before I Take the Sacrament," *Children's Songbook,* 73

Preparation

Make the dough for the pita bread earlier in the day. After it rises to twice its original size, punch it down and place it in the fridge. Obtain a picture of the sacrament trays or table for use in the lesson (see *Gospel Art Book,* 107, 108).

Lesson

Ask your family to be absolutely silent for a full minute. Time them, and watch them squirm. It will feel like the longest minute of their lives.

Now, ask them to get comfortable and choose a favorite song or story to focus on. Ask them to quietly think about their chosen topic or sing their favorite song in their mind for one minute. What difference did this minute make in their behavior?

Say the words *silence* and *reverence.* Ask your family to compare the meanings of the two words and decide how they are the same and how they are different. Show the picture of the sacrament trays or table and ask family members which word describes how we should act during this important ordinance.

There is a difference between being quiet and being reverent. Review the sacrament prayers as found in Doctrine and Covenants 20:56–57. Discuss the purpose of the sacrament and what we are asked to remember and think about while the prayers are being said and as the bread and water are being passed. Remind the family that the covenants we made at baptism are renewed every time we take the sacrament. Even before we come to sacrament meeting, we should be thinking about the Savior and how we can do better at keeping the commandments.

Talk about the types of songs that are sung before the sacrament prayers. Ask your family what the message of these songs is, why they help us feel reverent, and how they help us focus on the sacrament. Discuss family members' favorite sacrament hymns, and the feelings they bring. Ask for other ideas to help us focus on the purpose of the sacrament and be fully present in renewing our covenants.

Conclude by asking the family to again get comfortable and spend a quiet minute thinking about the lesson. Be mindful of the Spirit in the room and point out these feelings to the family. Encourage family members to prepare to partake of the sacrament each week by striving to keep the commandments and trying to be like Jesus Christ.

Activity

Hold a family sing-along. Sing each person's favorite song from *Hymns* or the *Children's Songbook*.

Treat

Pita Bread

1 cup warm water

2 teaspoons yeast

2 teaspoons salt

2 teaspoons olive oil

2 ½ cups flour

1. Pour the yeast into the warm water and let it sit until the yeast is dissolved.
2. Add the salt, oil, and flour. Work into the beginning stages of dough.
3. When the ingredients are fully mixed, turn out the dough and knead it for about five minutes to allow it to become smooth and elastic.
4. Grease the mixing bowl and return the dough to the bowl. Cover and let rise until double in size.
5. Gently punch down the dough and divide it into eight pieces. Flatten these into rounds like you would pizza dough, about ¼" thick.
6. Place the pitas on a warmed cookie sheet and bake for 3 minutes at 450°F.
7. Dip pieces of warm pita bread in honey butter or jam butter.

Additional Resources

Michelle Lehnardt, "The Most Important Part," *Friend,* June 2007. http://www.lds.org/friend/2007/06/the-most-important-part?lang=eng

"When I take the sacrament I renew my baptismal covenants," *Friend,* May 2012. http://www.lds.org/bc/content/shared/content/images/magazines/friend/2012/05/fr12may39-sacrament-coloring-page.pdf?lang=eng

Charlotte G. Lindstrom, "Sacrament," *Friend,* July 2001. http://www.lds.org/bc/content/ldsorg/children/resources/topics/sacrament/Sacrament-2001-07-friend.pdf?lang=eng

The Sabbath

Scripture

Doctrine and Covenants 59:9–10

Song

"When I Go to Church," *Children's Songbook,* 157

Preparation

Gather six sheets of construction paper and a marker. Draw one letter of the word *CHURCH* on each sheet, then scramble them.

Lesson

Begin handing the family your letters and asking them to decide what word they spell.

Lay out the letters on a surface where they can be easily seen. Discuss why it is important to go to our church meetings, which Heavenly Father has commanded us to do. Point out each letter and say that it represents something Heavenly Father would like us to accomplish when we go to our church meetings.

C: Connect with other Saints.
H: Honor Heavenly Father and Jesus Christ.
U: Understand the gospel.
R: Renew our covenants.
C: Challenge ourselves to do better.
H: Have peace.

How are these goals accomplished? What difference do they make in our lives, and how do they help us have stronger testimonies and be closer to Heavenly Father? What kinds of things can interfere with our ability or desire to attend our church meetings, and how can we overcome these obstacles?

Work together to create a list of things to do or prepare on Saturday to help the family feel the Holy Ghost in their church meetings on Sunday, as well as at home.

Remind the family that Heavenly Father has asked us not only to attend our church meetings, but to honor and set aside the entire Sunday as His day. Begin a discussion about other things that can be done to honor the Sabbath and turn it into a special day. Refer back the reasons you listed for going to church. What activities can help you continue to reach these goals for the rest of the day?

Remind the family that in a very busy world, the Sabbath day is not about "I can't," but rather "I can." It is a day for remembering what matters most and refocusing on those things, a day for finding peace and re-establishing a strong connection with Heavenly Father so you can navigate the rest of the week with faith, energy, and confidence. The other days of the week can feel as if you are a child faced with a plate of unpleasant vegetables. Sundays are dessert—they are sweet and enjoyable and shouldn't be rushed (or mixed with vegetables).

Activity

Hold relay races with old church clothes to see who can get ready for "church" the fastest.

Treat

Sundaes

Additional Resources

Benjamin De Hoyos, "A Truckload of Saints," *Liahona*, Sept. 2007. http://www.lds.org/liahona/2007/09/a-truckload-of-saints?lang=eng

Julie Wardell, "Doing Good on the Sabbath Day," *Liahona,*
    Sept. 2007. http://www.lds.org/liahona/2007/09/for-
    little-friends/doing-good-on-the-sabbath-day?lang=eng
"Flannel Board Sunday Box," *Liahona,* June 2006. http://www.
    lds.org/liahona/2006/06/flannel-board-sunday-box?lang=eng
"Getting Ready for Church," *Friend,* Sept. 2009. http://www.
    lds.org/bc/content/shared/content/images/gospel-library/
    magazine/fr09sep35_search.jpg?lang=eng

Tithing

Scripture

Doctrine and Covenants 97:12

Song

"I Want to Give the Lord My Tenth," *Children's Songbook,* 150

Preparation

Gather some loose change, a piece of paper, and a pencil.

Lesson

Show a single dime or other coin and ask the family to consider all the things they could do with it. Is it enough to buy a piece of candy? Save for something later? Place in a donation jar? Remind the family that when we obey the law of tithing, the money we give will bless our own life and the lives of others.

Heavenly Father has blessed us with many great things. In return, He asks us to show our gratitude by returning a portion—ten percent—to Him. Then, He uses it to bless us and other people. Paying even the smallest amount of tithing will fill us with gratitude and faith.

Use the questions below and on the next page to review what the family knows about tithing. For each right answer, let the person who answered name an amount of money. Use the piece of paper to write down the amounts. Then, show the family how to "hop" the decimal point one place to the left as an easy way to calculate how much tithing should be paid on that dollar amount.

- How much are we supposed to pay in tithing?
- What color is the envelope your tithing goes into?

- To whom do we give the tithing at church?
- Name one thing tithing pays for.
- Spell *tithing*.
- Who can pay tithing?
- Do we get anything back when we pay our tithing?
- Name another type of donation listed on the tithing slip.
- Has tithing always been paid with money?
- What does a percent sign look like?
- Who counts and records your money for the Church records?
- Whose face is on the penny? Dime? One-dollar bill?

Explain that great or small, our tithing helps with important things, such as building Church meetinghouses and temples. All of our tithing counts and brings great blessings.

Activity

Gather all the change you can find in the house and use it to work together to make a mosaic of a chapel or temple.

Treat

Serve penny candy. Let the family trade in their remaining pennies from the activity for small pieces of individual treats, such as M&Ms, jelly beans, marshmallows, or chocolate chips.

Additional Resources

Matt and Mandy, "Paying Tithing," *Friend*, Sept. 2010. http://www.lds.org/friend/online-activities/videos/matt-mandy?lang=eng#paying-tithing

Chad E. Phares, "Just One Coin," *Liahona,* Aug. 2001. http://media.ldscdn.org/pdf/lds-magazines/liahona-august-2011/2011-08-28-for-young-children-eng.pdf

"Where Does Tithing Go?" *Liahona*, Sept. 2005. http://www.lds.org/liahona/2005/09/for-little-friends?lang=eng

Callie Buys, "Tithing Around the World," *Friend*, June 2006. http://www.lds.org/friend/2006/06/funstuf/tithing-around-the-world?lang=eng

"Chapter 44: Tithing (July 1838)," Doctrine and Covenants Stories, lds.org. http://www.lds.org/media-library/video/doctrine-and-covenants/doctrine-and-covenants-stories?lang=eng#2010-06-45-chapter-44-tithing-july-1838

The Word of Wisdom

Scripture

Doctrine and Covenants 89:4

Song

"The Word of Wisdom," *Children's Songbook,* 154

Preparation

Gather several grocery store ads, a small piece of poster board, scissors, and glue.

Lesson

Begin by asking the family to recall a time when they have truly enjoyed being active and healthy (playing with friends, excelling at a sport, or simply enjoying their body's wonderful capabilities). Now, have them compare that to a time when they were ill. What was wrong? What things couldn't they do? How did their thoughts and attitudes change? Even when they started getting better, how long was it before they felt as good as they had in the healthy example?

Coming to earth and getting a physical body is a privilege because it allows us to one day become like Heavenly Father. How is this goal affected when we make choices that can harm our physical body? How we feel physically affects how we feel spiritually. We all get sick and experience different trials, but if we love and respect our bodies and try to keep them healthy, when sickness does come we will be able to recover more easily.

Heavenly Father gave us the Word of Wisdom to help us take care of our bodies. Discuss some of the parts of the Word of Wisdom. How could the things we are told to avoid affect our bodies? How would this, in turn, effect our spirits? How do the things we are told to do affect our bodies and spirits?

Show the family the grocery ads. Look through them together and choose things to "buy" for a day of healthy living. Cut out and discuss the family's choices as you glue the ads to the poster board in meal and snack clusters. Discuss ways to choose well-balanced meals and form good exercise habits, as well as how to avoid things that are bad for our bodies.

Activity

Take a family walk, or do another favorite physical activity.

Treat

Green Monkey Milkshake

1 cup milk
½ cup vanilla yogurt
1 banana, frozen
1–2 tablespoons peanut butter
2 cups fresh baby spinach
1 cup ice

Blend all the ingredients until smooth. (This recipe makes one serving for everyone to try a small amount.)

Additional Resources

Julie Wardell, "Good Choices," *Friend*, Oct. 2005. https://www.lds.org/friend/2005/10/good-choices?lang=eng

Amie Jane Leavitt, "Word of Wisdom Promise," *Friend*, Nov. 2006. http://www.lds.org/bc/content/shared/content/images/gospel-library/magazine/fr06nov07_funstuf.jpg?lang=eng

"God Gave Them Knowledge." lds.org. http://www.lds.org/media-library/video/2011-03-10-god-gave-them-knowledge?lang=eng

Ready for Baptism

Scripture
Doctrine and Covenants 68:27

Song
"I Like My Birthdays," *Children's Songbook,* 104

Preparation
Write the title of the first lesson in this book on two cards, then write the title of the second lesson on two cards, and so on with all of the lesson titles. When you finish, you should have 44 cards.

Lesson
Ask the family to list ways a person can know whether or not he or she is ready to be baptized. Remind the family that you have been working with your child during family home evening to help the child feel prepared and understand the covenants he or she will be making at baptism.

Another way the child will prepare is by meeting with the bishop. He will talk with the child about his or her testimony and help the child decide if he or she is ready to be baptized. The bishop does this by asking questions and getting to know the child. Some of his questions will include: Do you have a testimony of Heavenly Father and Jesus Christ? Do you know what it means to repent? Do you pay your tithing? Tell the child that these are all things you have been learning about in family home evening.

To help the child gain confidence in his or her own testimony and ability to answer the bishop's questions, show the child the cards you prepared. Shuffle them, then lay them out in a grid, face down, on a table or other flat surface. The family will play a memory game with the cards. Each person will take turns choosing two cards and turning them over, looking for a match. If the cards match, the person must state one thing he or she has learned about the topic on the cards, then remove them from the playing area. If the cards do not match, they are simply turned back over, and play continues with the next person. By the time the playing area is cleared, you will have reviewed everything you have been learning over the past few weeks, and your child will be ready to take the final steps to prepare for baptism.

Activity

Help the child preparing for baptism to make a list of everything he or she will need on baptism day. Then let the child pack his or her bag.

Treat

Bishop's Bread

1 egg
½ cup sugar
¼ cup vegetable oil
1 teaspoon vanilla
1 cup buttermilk
½ teaspoon salt
½ teaspoon baking soda
2 cups flour
½ cup chopped nuts
½ cup raisins
½ cup chocolate chips
½ cup chopped maraschino cherries

1. Blend the egg, sugar, and oil, then add the buttermilk and vanilla.
2. Stir together the flour, salt, and baking soda. Add to the wet mixture and combine well.
3. Fold in the nuts, raisins, chocolate, and cherries.
4. Bake in a greased 9" x 5" bread pan for 1 hour at 350°F.
5. Cool completely in the pan.
6. Don't forget to take a slice to your bishop when it's interview time!

Additional Resources

"What to Do Now?" *Liahona,* Oct. 2006. http://www.lds.org/liahona/2006/10/what-to-do-now?lang=eng

"Journey to Baptism," *Friend,* Oct. 2006. http://www.lds.org/bc/content/ldsorg/children/resources/topics/baptism/Journey-to-Baptism-2006-10-friend.pdf?lang=eng

Elise Black, "My Baptism Book," *Friend,* May 1996. http://www.lds.org/bc/content/ldsorg/children/resources/topics/baptism/My-Baptism-Book-1996-05-friend.pdf?lang=eng